ILLEGAL IMMIGRATION A ROAD TO LEGAL CITIZENSHIP BY BOB BRUNELLE

Illegal Immigration!
A Road To Legal Citizenship
by Bob Brunelle

Table of Contents

Table of Contents

1. Introduction

First thing I want you to know is that I am an ordinary Caucasian American citizen. The reason I tell you this is I want you to know this country needs great law abiding immigrants to be legal in this country. I'm sure you have heard the term "our immigration system is broken".

The 4 basic reasons why our immigration system is broken.

1. The so called do-gooders are the problem and they make the situation worse than it already is.

2. We are supposed to please everyone, as you can see by our present situation that doesn't work. We need to have a plan.

3. The government has made it so difficult and expensive to become a legal citizen that most illegal immigrants have given up.

4. The government keeps telling us it is impossible to fix illegal immigration and we are supposed to believe it. Nothing is impossible if you believe.

I am offering a commonsense approach. That's something most people with the power to change things are not using these days. You see it every day in this PC correct world.

Will everyone like this plan? I'm sure they won't. This plan will involve time and commitment. That's two things people can't deal with. People want everything free. They don't want to work for anything. They have been misled to believe that they are entitled to everything with no effort.

This plan will be a start to getting illegal immigration under control. This plan won't cost the US tax payer a dime. The government would fund this plan with 2 new ways of revenue.

1. The monthly application period fees.
2. Every illegal immigrant would start paying federal and state taxes.

Employers would have a new legal work force. The best thing about this plan is we will only be deporting the illegals that are bad for our country.

I am a proud American that only wants the best for this country. I believe that this country can be great again when we have great people contributing to the country's future. My definition of great people are people that give their best every day to God, Family and Country. I am talking about people that hold themselves accountable for their actions.

Thanks,
Bob Brunelle
A Concerned American Citizen.

2. Purpose of This Law

The purpose of this law is to:

1. Protect law bidding illegal immigrants and give them a road to legal American citizenship.

2. Protect law bidding illegal immigrants from ever being deported.

3. Instill self-deportation of all illegal immigrants that do not abide by our laws.

4. Deport all illegal immigrants that don't file and pay their federal and state income taxes.

5. Deport all illegal immigrants with a criminal record.

6. Inform illegal immigrants that when they come to this country they must abide by the laws of this country or be deported.

7. Inform immigrants that legal citizenship is possible and affordable but it will take time, effort and commitment on their part.

8. Keep the overpaid lawyers out of the immigration business.

9. Let illegal immigrants know that legal citizenship it is a privilege not a right and they must earn it and follow our laws.

10. Stop the deportation of millions of illegal immigrants that want to remain in this country legally.

3. The Road To Legal Citizenship

A. Illegal Immigrant: a person that has entered this country Illegal or has stayed in this country after their work visa has expired.

B. Registration period: a12 month period where all illegal Immigrants will be required to register with the Illegal immigration registration office so they may begin the path to legal immigration. This registration is designed to solve 3 major problems.
   a. Stop the deportation of illegal immigrants that want to become legal citizens and follow our laws.
   b. Allow for future immigrants with work visa that have expired to have an opportunity to become legal citizens.
   c. Secure the border as soon as possible using whatever means necessary.

C. Immigration registration office: Where all illegal Immigrants must register to begin their path to legal citizenship. Registration may be done in person or on line. When registration is completed the Illegal Immigrant status will change from Illegal Immigrant to Immigrant in process and a registration certificate will be issued.

D. Registered Immigrant: an illegal immigrant that has registered with the immigration registration office either in person or on line and has received a registration certificate.

E. Registration certificate: this certificate is proof that the illegal Immigrant has registered with the immigration registration office either in person or on line and is waiting for the background check to be completed so the registered immigrant start the application period.

F. Qualification period: the qualification period is for 60 months and begins after the following registered immigrant has completed the following steps.

1. A registration certificate has been issued.
2. A background check has been completed.
3. The registered immigrant has physically reported to the immigration registration office for photos and finger printing.
4. Registered Immigrants will be issued identification card.
5. A driver's license may be obtain stating that they are a registered immigrants in the qualification period
6. Driver's licenses will be issued to registered immigrants after completion of driver's

qualifications required by the state they reside in.

7. During the qualification period the registered immigrant must carry an identification card and driver's license at all times.

8. A monthly report form must completed on line or in person.

9. A reporting receipt will be issued after the monthly report has been completed.

10. A monthly registration fee based on income will be paid to the immigration registration office.

11. A yearly filed tax returned must be sent and approved by the immigration registration office in writing.

12. Learn to speak and write the English language. The application for citizenship will only be available in the English language.

G. Application period: The application period begins at the end of the fourth year of the qualification period and expires at the end of the qualification period. The application period is a onetime only period. The application period is the only time a registered immigrant will have the opportunity to apply for legal citizenship.

H. Probation period is for 36 months and begins on the day that registered immigrant has been granted legal citizenship. All right of a legal citizens will be granted.

4. Definition Of An Illegal Immigrant

1. Immigrants that do not register with the immigration registration office.

2. Immigrants that have a felony conviction.

3. Immigrants with an expired work visa that have not registered with the immigration registration office.

4. Registered immigrants that do not comply with the qualification period rules.

5. Registered immigrants that are convicted of a felony during the qualification period or probation period.

6. Immigrants that are deported.

7. Immigrants that have entered the United Stated illegally.

8. Immigrants that have entered the United Sated illegally will have lost their opportunity to be granted legal citizenship.

5. Legal Immigrant Children With Illegal Immigrant parents.

1. Any immigrant that cannot qualify for legal citizenship that have minor children that are legal citizens, may grant them custody to a legal US citizen guardian.

2. Illegal immigrants waiting to enter the United Sated legally will be granted a 48 hour visitation pass 4 times during a 12 month period starting 6 months after deportation.

3. No future passes will be granted if the illegal immigrant violates the rules of the visitation pass.

4. In the event a non-qualifying illegal immigrant does not have legal citizen guardians, the legal minor children will be deported with their parents.

5. Legal children of illegal immigrants may return to the US at the age of 18. They must register with the immigration registration office within 7 days of reentering the US and will be on a 3 year probation period.

6. Legal children of illegal immigrants reentering the US with a felony conviction will be not be allowed to reestablish legal citizenship and will be deported.

6. Illegal Immigrants That Have Been Deported

1. Illegal immigrants that report to the authorities for self-deportation will have 12 months for the day of deportation to apply to reenter the United Sated legally.

2. Illegal immigrants reentering the US legally must register with the immigration registration office within 7 business days to maintain their legal visa status.

3. Illegal immigrants deported by the authorities will be ineligible to reenter the US legally for a period of 36 months from the date of deportation.

4. Illegal immigrants that are deported with a felony conviction are not illegible to become legal US citizens.

5. Illegal immigrants entering the US illegally are not illegible to become US citizens.

7. Objections and Solutions

Illegal immigrants often complain that to become a legal citizen it is very expensive and they have to hire lawyers to do it right. I totally agree even the politicians agree that our road to legal citizenship is broken. I hear stories where hard working honest illegal immigrants have been taken advantage of by unscrupulous lawyers and con artist.

What I am proposing is s affordable solution and no 3rd party person like a lawyer will be needed. This will help eliminate the chances of an illegal immigrant being taken advantage of by unscrupulous people.

All illegal immigrants will be required to go thru the same process regardless of their financial status. I don't think we should start discriminating against illegal immigrants before they even have a chance to become a legal citizen.

1. It's too expensive to implement:

   - All applicants will pay a fee for 60 months. If a $100.00 a month on average fee is paid these are the numbers.
   - Multiply that by 7 million (II) that is a total of $420,000,000 or $84,000,000 per year to the government or a private company to pay for this program.
   - A private company would do it better and cheaper with new jobs in the private sector.

- All registered immigrants will now have to start filling and paying their taxes like all legal citizens. More revenue will be generated to the government
- Employers will have more eligible employees to expand their companies. That will help our sagging economy.

That covers all the cost with some profit for the government.

2. It's too difficult:

- It's very doable with today's technology.
- We want to make immigrants work for their citizenship.
- This will discourage more immigrants from entering our country illegally.

3. This won't work because the border is not secure:

- We only need to secure the border during the initial registration period.
- After the registration period deadline, all immigrants that did not register to the immigration registration office will be deemed as an illegal immigrant and will be deported.

Some critics will say this will never work. We can't please everyone we all see what happens when we try to please everyone. I think all law abiding illegal immigrants are caught in the middle of our incompetent leaders that have no clue what to do and are afraid to do anything if they did.

This plan is affordable both for the illegal immigrant and the US. This plan won't discourage the immigrants from following are laws. The only immigrants that will be discourage is the immigrants that are not interested in the wellbeing of this country. We don't want them in this country.

We need law abiding immigrants to follow our laws and help make our country great again.

I know it will work and it's the only real plan we have.

Thanks for reading this book.
Bob Brunelle a concerned American citizen.

Notes

Notes

Notes

Notes

Notes

www.ingramcontent.com/pod-product-compliance
Lightning Source LLC
Chambersburg PA
CBHW070259300526
45791CB00022B/1668